SMALL PORCELAIN HEAD

Also by Allison Benis White

Self-Portrait with Crayon

SMALL PORCELAIN HEAD

Allison Benis White

Four Way Books
Tribeca

for Nicole

Please direct all inquiries to:
Editorial Office
Four Way Books
POB 535, Village Station
New York, NY 10014
www.fourwaybooks.com

Library of Congress Cataloging-in-Publication Data

White, Allison Benis, 1972-
  Small porcelain head / Allison Benis White.
      p. cm.
  Poems.
  ISBN 978-1-935536-27-7 (pbk. : alk. paper)
  I. Title.
  PS3623.H569S63 2013
  811'.6--dc23
                                        2012029325

This book is manufactured in the United States of America
and printed on acid-free paper.

Four Way Books is a not-for-profit literary press. We are grateful for the assistance
we receive from individual donors, public arts agencies, and private foundations.

Funding for this book was provided in part by a generous donation
in memory of John J. Wilson.

[clmp] We are a proud member
        of the Council of Literary Magazines and Presses.

Distributed by University Press of New England
One Court Street, Lebanon, NH 03766

Contents

•

••

•••

If pain is only weakness leaving the body,
black curls, still wet, painted on her fore-
head.

If pain is a desire for dark shapes, even
when dried, glistening, if you are reading
this.

What is left but obsession, handling the object over and over? My hands fit around her waist.

Unbuttoning, I wanted nothing to happen or the same thing to happen forever in the same place.

Although it is better, it is impossible to miss one thing or when you go, to miss yourself.

Soon the object must grow or become invisible, so familiar it is so hollow you are inside.

I have lost all hope for myself, she wrote, meaning there is one coat left which has failed.

We have already undressed. Once I thought what could happen was only what I could imagine.

Please forgive me. I pray and can't make it
stop. There were lambswool wigs and paper-
weight eyes, two factory fires. Instead of
blankness, I learned to draw stars with two
triangles, one upside down and overlapping
the other. I covered pages, then like brace-
lets, my wrists.

That she has the right to turn the room inward. That when I speak, ashes flutter from my mouth.

That her hands are drawn in lipstick on the mirror, two firecrackers. That her hands are gone.

I cannot go any further with my mind. That my mind is a hole, when it flickers, means *bang*.

Even the violence is sentimental, limbs and head unstrung, not blood but wings, red butterfly, a glass box, a thousand pins, the end.

Or clear red ovals lowered into a jar and coiled, a head on a neck made of rubies, a hive—God does not make sense, is never quiet.

And she would talk when the string was pulled, without opening her mouth, just a voice from a record, a slot in the side of her chest.

I would want her to whisper, to start from the beginning, repeating one sentence that is true: *I know this will come as a shock to you.*

Not to let go or have to—her face seems scraped, like the knee of a child, a pattern of thin red lines.

Love her roughly or leave her alone for days, years—indestructible, not a cloth head filled with cotton.

I left a sweater on a train in Dover last fall—if I would have shivered, noticed emptiness or shoulders.

If there is no God, only white streamers left over from evening, collected like women who have fainted.

Buttoned together at their hips and shoulders and heads, when the cord is yanked, the cloth couple must dance violently, without the threat of consummation or injury, as death augments intimacy, ends the need for partitions, as they cannot get close enough to each other now (because they are not afraid) because there is no future.

After our fingers, we put our mouths to the pain—a ceramic tongue broken off like chalk.

As I child, I pressed my tongue to my wrist to see what it would be like to feel some-one.

What should I do with my mind? Think of the way it broke until the breaking is language.

••

If description is a living thing, dark cherry hair and glass eyes, tilted away—I want to say something that will look at me.

If to memorize is to adore and cannot afford distraction or a socket neck that rotates the head away, if death is turning away, with long, brown human hair, revolving like a globe, from every angle, the back of her head.

Just as the cork descends from the neck to permit a release from pulling—the body in one hand, head in the other—separation is revelation.

Just as the body is now headless, waiting— as if the motive to live was loneliness, the body remembers a head, opens its arms romantically:

I live to miss you.

Unlike the other automatons who lift a hand mirror or balloon, she exists even when we close our eyes, slapping one small brass cymbal into another, frantically, to prove touching.

The arm is wood and narrows into the wrist, small as I want—to have one thing I love carved from everything.

A wooden hand is a hand without finger-nails, sanded palm and the color of skin, an oar rowing in air.

Then a windmill, from the hand. As in human profiles cut into trees with a knife, two people sailing.

When I have a headache, I lift my hand over my eyes—if death is a failure of imagin-ation, we are alive.

If God is everything, then he is this empti-
ness and eyelids that close when her head is
tipped back in the dark and click. If God
is nothing.

Click. But quiet as the last number or a
bubble risen to the surface that breaks just
before a face pushes through the water and
breathes.

Pinholes in her plastic chest that formed the outline of a star, so there was something to touch.

Or the brush she came with—its thin handle and small oval back, and each bristle, like pleading.

I was asking for something. I could cut out the star of my chest, I thought, stop keeping.

Cutting her black hair into a jagged bob with utility scissors when I was five. And afterward, when I wanted it back, I thought it would take weeks, months. But then, unevenly framed around her face, I understood time was done.

Only her eyes, which cause us to feel em-
pathy.

The mutual helplessness of seeing and being
seen.

Looking where the mouth should be is no
help.

Now that the paint has worn off she has
none.

Which pulls the focus back to the eyes'
conversation.

· · ·

She pushes the white metal carriage, real-
izes the baby is gone. Each time the key in
her back is turned, she takes a few steps,
knows again. Because she can only move
inches at a time, it is a small story. And the
same. A gasp really. No one should ever turn
the key. But this would be cruel: naive,
sedentary.

What we end up with in the end or sooner, both brows and lashes indicated by a series of nicks.

Awaiting execution, Marie Antoinette made a wooden doll, still preserved in a museum in England.

That kind of making. Carved until the mind is a doll of a woman in a wooden cell making a doll.

One evening as a child, before I went to bed, I called the operator and said my house is on fire.

Decapitated, there would not be much time to discern the greater ease—thoughtlessness or nothing.

Of those who survived their attempts, just after they tried, many said they changed their minds.

As with every revelation, midair, oblivion is realigned and clarified: I want to die then decide.

This is the gift of violence: the head is dropped and broken so the world can get out.

But the world grew inside her again and would not calm down—a swollen metal whistle.

Split open against the wall, the world was released from her head again, but I am worried.

An entire story on one body, a brass knob,
a head, when turned, my finger hooked
around the neck, and the girl becomes the
wolf in a velvet hood, the red felt tongue set
to mean better to eat you than sleep, better
to never be.

How the stillness keeps expanding in the
skull.

And the original thin blue cap nailed to her
scalp.

It hurts to think of anyone tied to the earth
with twine.

My hair grows longer and longer, trying to
leave.

For the easily broken heads of bisque or china, tin heads, made separately, cut and stamped from sheet metal, welded together, then painted or enameled in Saxony, now in boxes, on bodies dressed in black or maroon capes with fur collars, each shattered head exchanged for a metal one but it is not enough.

The miracle is rooted in contrast, from *miraculum*, object of wonder, as in to look then believe. I want to conceive what I see: one glass-blown green eye, one gray, cracked—my mind, my mind can be changed. Please stay. In the repair shop window display, a face half-deteriorated, half-sane.

• • • •

Several leather fingers have now been reattached and folded in her lap, just as I wanted to live but could not stand my mind anymore. Because the desire to make and to cease are equal, when I'm still, I lace my fingers together to make the shape of a small head.

Each time she taps the egg, the top opens to reveal a glass-eyed monkey. I don't know why. It is better when it goes back inside. When the shell is smooth and off-white, not yet touched. God only wants one thing: to multiply.

Legs apart and arms extended, trimmed
with gold boots, to make dolls out of death
is to make children.

In a glass case, twenty-nine, clearly por-
celain in the mind: a smooth white forehead,
how ice cubes fail.

The point is to count silently. I tap one
finger on my thigh. Three with bathtubs,
ten light-blue eyes.

If I could remember, I would not count
them—if there was time, I would not need
children, or a mind.

Twins in red silk dresses, in case one is lost or damaged. Because it will happen, because there are two. Preparation covets disaster: one kept in a box under the bed, one seated on the dresser in a wire chair. Someday they will both be gone and I will be able to dream without images, rooms. Love for the world—I look at her sitting, check under the bed—is ruin.

A mechanism in the body controls the mouth, opening when her stomach is pressed: *I speak because I am touched, wearing a white baby's dress.*

No, she is mute as the moments I accept God or make a voice from objects, pressing her stomach, pressing her stomach, not screaming.

Or lost teeth kept in a ring box, collected in the red velvet depression, to open my mouth.

Sewn together at the waist, two torsos—one brown cloth, one cream. In other words, this is the conflict of pregnancy: when her skirt is lifted, Mary is delivered from Marie. And the reverse, later, because she requires company. I could say birth, when one leaves the other headfirst, in-between. Or the moment after the other face is covered, when there is no more mother, no relief—only Mary, dizzy from loneliness, symmetry.

What makes the object alive is desire without relief.

There is no time for a voice box or asking why.

Some things cannot be helped—God, double jeopardy.

Hold your face up to the light although you do not see.

Hold the body up to the lamp although you do not believe.

Although it does not breathe, it is getting warmer.

· · · · ·

Wax is most like skin, often perspiring and pliant, the forehead clear and thinking of ending.

If I could tell you everything now with the fluency of dying—I am not what happened to me.

Including the body, at the right temperature, everything melts into the conclusion of myth.

Drawn on paper then buried in a bottle in my backyard, an image of a girl's face softening.

Although terror mirrors awe in human expression.

Her parted lips and disheveled dark-blonde hair.

Either way, we understand, she is no longer fair.

Within the bonnet, the two-faced head is rotated by pulling a string from the torso: one face calm, one crying plastic beads on her cheeks—turning: peaceful, sad, peaceful, sad.

Nothing in-between, no transition—I don't remember why she is suffering, why she is glad. It happens so fast: I am hopeless as I pull the string in her torso, then sick with wonder.

Because the pain is company. Because the operator activates the body like a glove puppet.

Because the novelty wears off quickly and the hand, withdrawn, leaves the body exhausted.

Because to live is to be entered vertically and repeatedly, the pain is love and making me.

Is this the beauty that is made from suffering?

An open mouth with a visible trembling tongue.

Or is this just suffering, through witness, glorified?

My mouth is carved open, painted red as evidence.

Then the relief when the accordion of bodies opens. Meaning alone, to never have been. Just the thinness of their heads and the shape of wrists, seamless as the place they were cut from, where God means you are no one.

We call the denial of stillness *resurrection*—
a key turned, moaning, in the back of her
head.

We keep asking *but is it true?* And then if
anything is true, when her arms lift and
open.

After a while, we moan and lift our arms
in order to feel what she feels: her pose is
agony.

And when she is held closer, two blue eyes and a closed mouth, painted to imply dimension. With a hot washcloth, her face could be cleaned featureless. And turned on her stomach afterward, the seam that runs from the top of her neck to the bottom of her spine could be pulled open to say *release, quiet.*

Made with a hollow in the body to accept
a stand rod, the emptiness is explained and
a nest.

Even a hole in a plastic mouth, made to fit
a bottle, as her head was cupped and tilted
back.

Or feathers pulled from a rip in a pillow,
until the opposite is the same: she is empty
enough.

Now filled with sand and placed on the bed—if the wind blew or a door shut, she would stay.

By the time you read this, the letter began, someone has already called out, opened the door.

Now her hair brushed, now my head resting on her chest—now her body in a paper dress.

Acknowledgments

Grateful acknowledgment is made to the editors of
publications in which some of these poems first appeared:
*The American Poetry Review, Copper Nickel, The Laurel Review,
New Orleans Review,* and *Ploughshares.*

I would like to warmly thank The San Francisco Foundation
for selecting the first portion of *Small Porcelain Head* for the
James D. Phelan Award, and Claudia Rankine for selecting
this collection for the Four Way Books Levis Prize in Poetry.

Allison Benis White's poems have appeared in
The American Poetry Review, *The Iowa Review*, and *Ploughshares*,
among other journals. Her honors include the *Indiana Review*
Poetry Prize, *Prairie Schooner's* Bernice Slote Award, and a
Writers Exchange Award from *Poets & Writers*. She
is the author of *Self-Portrait with Crayon*, winner of the
Cleveland State University Poetry Center First Book Prize.
She teaches at the University of California, Irvine.